August 2013

NEXT GENERATION JAMMER

DOD Should Continue to Assess Potential Duplication and Overlap As Program Moves Forward

NEXT GENERATION JAMMER

DOD Should Continue to Assess Potential Duplication and Overlap As Program Moves Forward

Highlights of GAO-13-642, a report to congressional committees

Why GAO Did This Study

At an estimated cost of over $7 billion, the Navy's NGJ program represents a significant investment in airborne electronic attack capabilities. Jammers, like the planned NGJ, fly on aircraft, such as Navy EA-18Gs, and transmit electronic signals that can neutralize or temporarily degrade enemy air defenses and communications, thus aiding combat aircraft and ground forces' freedom to maneuver and strike. Senate Report 112-196 mandated GAO to review the NGJ program and potential duplication. This report examines the extent to which (1) DOD assessed whether there is duplication among NGJ, existing capabilities, and other acquisition programs, and (2) NGJ is being managed as a joint solution. GAO reviewed key NGJ requirements and acquisition documents and DOD and military service documents describing airborne electronic attack capabilities.

What GAO Recommends

To help ensure that DOD's analysis of potential overlap and duplication is complete, GAO recommends that the Secretary of Defense: (1) require the NGJ capability development document to discuss potential redundancies between NGJ and existing and proposed programs across all of its planned roles and (2) ensure that the Electronic Warfare Strategy Report to Congress includes information on potentially overlapping capabilities and why that overlap is warranted. DOD agreed to continue to assess duplication and redundancies but not with using the capability development document to do so. GAO believes the recommendation remains valid as discussed in the report. DOD agreed with the second recommendation.

View GAO-13-642. For more information, contact Michael J. Sullivan, (202) 512-4841, sullivanm@gao.gov.

What GAO Found

The Department of Defense (DOD) has assessed whether the planned Next Generation Jammer (NGJ) program is duplicative using a variety of means, but none of them address all of the system's planned roles or take into account the military services' evolving airborne electronic attack investment plans. DOD analyses support its conclusion that the NGJ meets a valid need and is not duplicative of existing capabilities in its primary role—suppressing enemy air defenses from outside the range of known surface-to-air missiles. However, these analyses do not address all planned NGJ roles, such as communications jamming in irregular warfare environments, or take into account the military services' evolving airborne electronic attack investment plans. According to GAO's analysis, none of the systems that have emerged since DOD completed its NGJ analyses duplicate its planned capabilities; however there is some overlap in the roles they are intended to perform. Redundancy in some of these areas may, in fact, be desirable. However, pursuing multiple acquisition efforts to develop similar capabilities can result in the same capability gap being filled twice or more, lead to inefficient use of resources, and contribute to other warfighting needs going unfilled. Therefore, continued examination of potential overlap and duplication among these investments may be warranted.

DOD has several ongoing efforts that could provide a mechanism for updating its analysis of potential overlap and duplication to address these shortcomings as the program moves forward. However, GAO found weaknesses in two of these efforts as well.

- **Electronic Warfare Strategy Report to Congress:** DOD could address new duplication issues as they emerge and, if necessary, explain the need for overlapping capabilities in this report. However, to date, the analysis of overlap and duplication in this report has been limited and did not examine potential overlap between capabilities or explain why overlap was warranted.
- **NGJ Capability Development Document:** Redundancies are required to be considered when a capability development document—which defines the performance requirements for an acquisition program—is validated. The draft NGJ capability development document does not identify the systems the Navy considered when analyzing potential redundancies, so it is difficult to evaluate whether its analysis includes existing and proposed programs across all of the NGJ's planned roles.

The NGJ is not being managed as a joint acquisition program, which is a distinction related to funding, but it is expected to provide the Navy with airborne electronic capabilities that will support all military services in both major combat operations and irregular warfare environments. The NGJ's capabilities are not intended to meet all of the military services' airborne electronic attack needs and the services are planning to make additional investments in systems that are tailored to meet their specific warfighting roles. The military services might be able to leverage the NGJ program in support of their own acquisition priorities because it plans to use a modular open systems approach, which allows for components to be added, removed, or modified without significantly impacting the rest of the system. This approach could make it easier to integrate the NGJ or its technologies into other systems in the future.

_____ **United States Government Accountability Office**

Contents

Abbreviations

AESA	Active Electronically Scanned Array
DOD	Department of Defense
GAO	Government Accountability Office
JCIDS	Joint Capabilities Integration and Development System
MALD-J	Miniature Air Launched Decoy—Jammer
NGJ	Next Generation Jammer
RDT&E	Research, development, test and evaluation

August 20, 2013

The Honorable Richard J. Durbin
Chairman
The Honorable Thad Cochran
Ranking Member
Subcommittee on Defense
Committee on Appropriations
United States Senate

The Honorable C.W. Bill Young
Chairman
The Honorable Pete Visclosky
Ranking Member
Subcommittee on Defense
Committee on Appropriations
House of Representatives

Airborne electronic attack capabilities are key enablers for U.S. military operations ranging from irregular warfare to major combat against potential near-peer adversaries.[1] Airborne electronic attack involves the use of aircraft to neutralize, destroy, or temporarily degrade (suppress) enemy air defense and communications systems, either through destructive or disruptive means. It helps protect aircraft, maritime, and ground forces from a variety of threats. For example, during major combat operations, airborne electronic attack helps prevent other systems, such as fighter jets or naval carriers, from being detected by enemy radars and targeted by missiles. In irregular warfare environments, it supports ground troops by performing functions such as jamming enemy communications. Weapons designed to counter U.S. airborne electronic attack capabilities are becoming increasingly common and sophisticated. These weapons—

---

[1]Irregular warfare is a violent struggle among state and non-state actors for legitimacy and influence over the relevant population(s). It favors indirect and asymmetric (dissimilar) approaches, though it may employ the full range of military and other capacities in order to erode an adversary's power, influence, and will.

Potential near-peer adversaries include countries capable of waging large-scale conventional war on the United States. These nation-states can be characterized as having nearly comparable diplomatic, informational, military, and economic capacity to the United States.

held by both nation-state and non-state actors—vary from advanced, integrated air defense systems to older surveillance radars that are being upgraded with advanced computers.

One of the current systems used to counter these threats is the AN/ALQ-99 (ALQ-99), a jamming pod system that operates from EA-6B Prowler and EA-18G Growler aircraft. Jammers transmit electronic signals that neutralize or temporarily degrade enemy air defenses and communications, thus aiding combat aircraft, maritime, and ground forces' freedom to maneuver and strike. According to the Department of Defense (DOD), the capabilities of the ALQ-99 are insufficient to keep up with rapidly evolving threats and the system is becoming obsolete. As a result, the Navy is planning to replace the ALQ-99 with a more capable Next Generation Jammer (NGJ) on its EA-18G aircraft. The NGJ program was authorized to begin technology development in July 2013, and the Navy expects the program to cost over $7 billion, including over $3 billion for research, development, test and evaluation, and over $4 billion for procurement.

Each of the military departments is making investments in airborne electronic attack capabilities. In March 2012, we found potential overlap among airborne electronic attack systems in development,[2] particularly among systems used for irregular warfare that the services were acquiring under urgent operational needs processes.[3] While some redundancy is often desirable, our prior work has shown that pursuing multiple acquisition efforts to develop similar capabilities can result in the same capability gap being filled twice or more, lead to inefficient use of resources, and contribute to other warfighting needs going unfilled.

We also found that DOD's ability to identify department-wide needs and solutions and eliminate potentially unnecessary overlap may have been undermined by a lack of designated, joint leadership charged with overseeing electronic warfare acquisition activities. Senate Report 112-196,[4] which accompanied the bill for the Department of Defense

---

[2]Overlap occurs when multiple agencies or programs have similar goals, engage in similar activities or strategies to achieve them, or target similar beneficiaries.

[3]GAO, *Airborne Electronic Attack: Achieving Mission Objectives Depends on Overcoming Acquisition Challenges,* GAO-12-175 (Washington, D.C.: Mar. 29, 2012).

[4]S. REP. No. 112-196, at 191 (2012).

Appropriations Act, 2013 and was subsequently incorporated into the Consolidated and Further Continuing Appropriations Act, 2013, directed GAO to review the NGJ program and potential duplication.[5] This report examines (1) the extent to which DOD has assessed whether there is duplication among the NGJ, existing capabilities, and other acquisition programs,[6] and (2) the extent to which the NGJ is being managed as a joint solution that supports multiple military services.

To determine the extent to which DOD assessed duplication among the NGJ, existing capabilities, and other acquisition programs, we reviewed key NGJ and DOD electronic warfare documents, including the 2004 Airborne Electronic Attack Initial Capabilities Document, the 2009 Electronic Warfare Initial Capabilities Document, the NGJ Analysis of Alternatives, and the DOD's annual Electronic Warfare Strategy Report to Congress. We assessed DOD's analysis of duplication against DOD's Joint Capabilities Integration and Development System (JCIDS) Manual. We also analyzed information provided by the military services regarding the capabilities and missions of existing and planned airborne electronic attack systems, and interviewed DOD, military service, program, and Joint Staff officials. To determine the extent to which the NGJ is being managed as a joint solution, we reviewed key requirements and acquisition documents reflecting military service and Joint Staff input into NGJ requirements and the acquisition program.[7] We also reviewed the NGJ Analysis of Alternatives and interviewed DOD, military service, program, and Joint Staff officials to determine whether the NGJ is intended to be used on multiple platforms.

We conducted this performance audit from November 2012 to August 2013 in accordance with generally accepted government auditing standards. Those standards require that we plan and perform the audit to obtain sufficient, appropriate evidence to provide a reasonable basis for our findings and conclusions based on our audit objectives. Our analysis was limited to information classified no higher than SECRET, but we

---

[5]Pub. L. No. 113-6 (2012).

[6]Duplication occurs when two or more agencies or programs are engaged in the same activities or provide the same services to the same beneficiaries.

[7]According to DOD Joint Publication 1-02, the term "joint" connotes activities, operations, organizations, etc. in which elements of two or more military departments participate.

believe that the evidence obtained provides a reasonable basis for our findings and conclusions based on our audit objectives.

Background

The NGJ is DOD's program to replace the ALQ-99 tactical jamming system. The ALQ-99 is a five-pod jamming system that is capable of automatically processing, and jamming radio frequency signals. It counters a variety of threats in low-, mid-, and high-band frequency ranges. Figure 1 shows the radars that operate in different frequency bands and ranges.

Figure 1: Radars Operating in Different Frequency Bands and Ranges

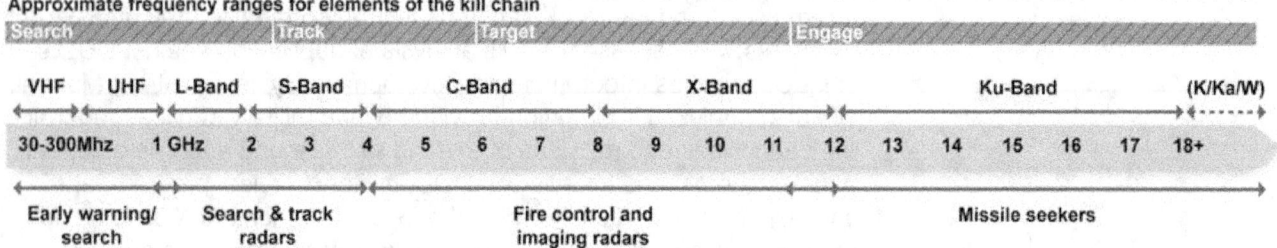

Source: GAO analysis of Massachusetts Institute of Technology Lincoln Laboratory, Navy, and National Telecommunications and Information Administration documents.

The ALQ-99 was originally flown on EA-6B aircraft, which are expected to be fully retired in 2019, and is transitioning to the EA-18G, an electronic attack variant of the Navy's F/A-18 fighter jet. Figure 2 shows the ALQ-99 on the EA-18G.

Figure 2: EA-18G with Three ALQ-99 Jamming Pods

ALQ-99

Source: U.S. Navy.

EA-6B and EA-18Gs can be based on aircraft carriers or in expeditionary squadrons that are deployed to land-based locations as needed. The ALQ-99/EA-6B combination was originally developed for use in major combat operations, and in 1995, the EA-6B was selected to become the sole tactical radar support jammer for all services after the Air Force decided to retire its fleet of EF-111 aircraft. The role of the EA-6B has continued to expand over time. According to DOD officials, when Operation Iraqi Freedom began, EA-6Bs were used in irregular warfare environments along with another aircraft, the EC-130H Compass Call, because they provided needed jamming capabilities and there were no other airborne electronic attack assets available for this role. These and other demands have strained DOD's airborne electronic attack capacity and increased the stress on systems, such as the ALQ-99.

Like the ALQ-99, the NGJ will be comprised of jamming pods that will fly on the Navy's EA-18G. Its main purpose will be to counter integrated air defense systems in major combat operations. The EA-18G with NGJ is to primarily be based on aircraft carriers at sea where it is to be employed in U.S. Navy carrier strike groups to counter both sea- and land-based weapon systems. DOD also plans for it to support joint expeditionary warfare missions. The EA-18G with NGJ is currently planned to primarily serve in a modified escort role, in which it is expected to jam enemy radars while the aircraft is outside the range of known surface-to-air missiles. It is also expected to be capable of conducting stand-off jamming missions, in which the aircraft is located outside of defended airspace. In both cases, the idea is to protect or "hide" other systems from enemy radars. The EA-18G with the NGJ is also intended to be used for other purposes, such as communications jamming. Figure 3 shows the NGJ with other airborne electronic attack systems countering enemy air defense systems.

Figure 3: Notional Depiction of Airborne Electronic Attack Systems Countering Enemy Air Defenses

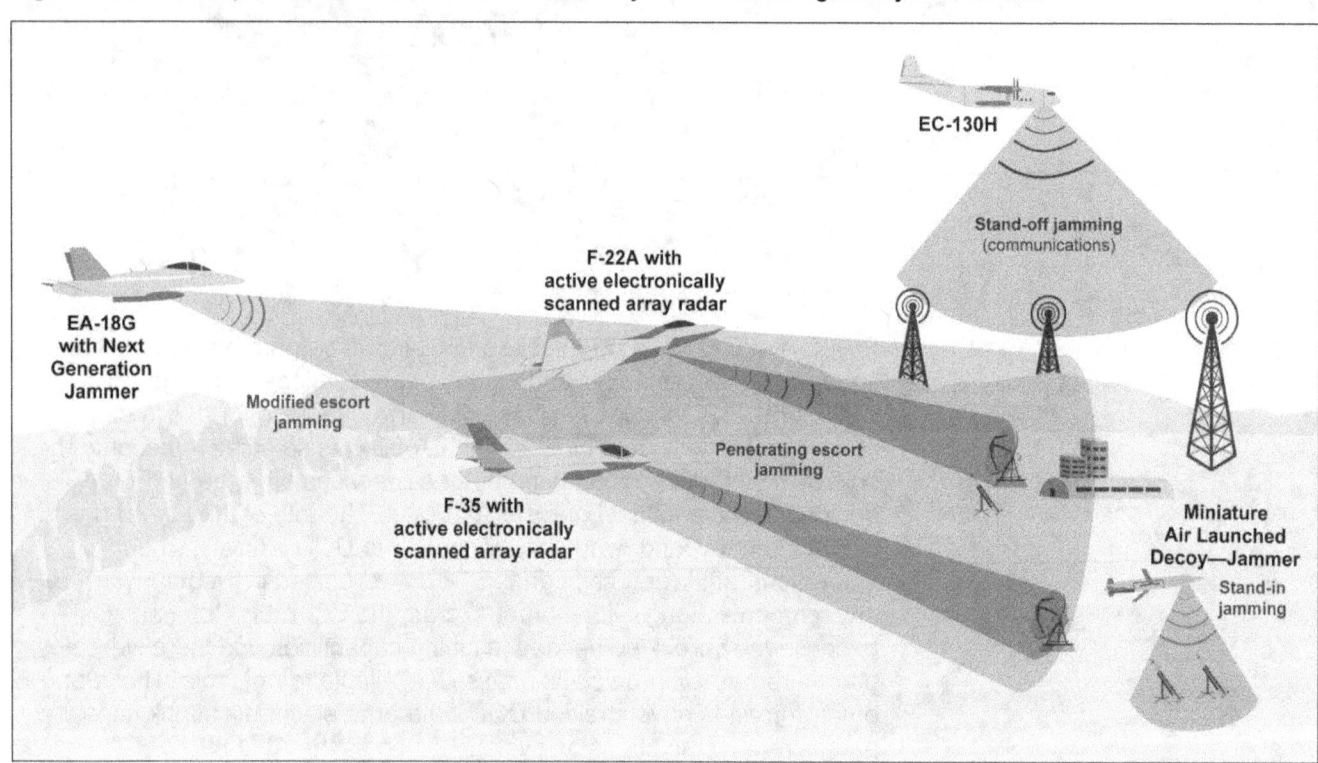

Sources: GAO (presentation); Boeing (EA-18G); Raytheon (Miniature Air Launched Decoy—Jammer); Lockheed Martin (F-35); Department of Defense (EC-130H and F-22A); Art Explosion (all other images).

Notes: Stand-off jamming occurs outside defended airspace.
Modified escort jamming occurs outside the known surface-to-air missile range.
Penetrating escort jamming occurs within known surface-to-air missile range.
Stand-in jamming occurs within the surface-to-air missile "no escape" zone.

In July 2013, DOD conducted a milestone A review for the NGJ program, which is a planned major defense acquisition program, and authorized it to enter the technology development phase.[8] Subsequent to the milestone A review, the Navy awarded a $279.4 million contract to Raytheon for NGJ technology development.[9] Figure 4 shows the time line for the milestone A review and other key NGJ events.

Figure 4: Time Line of Key NGJ Events

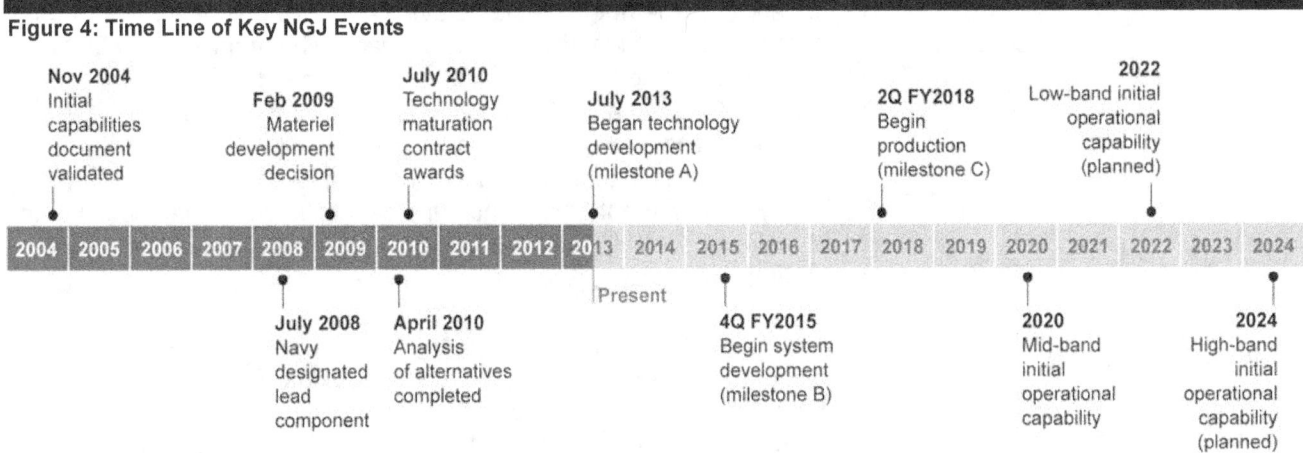

Source: GAO analysis of DOD documents and interview with DOD officials.

The NGJ program plans to use an incremental approach to development in which the most critical capabilities are to be delivered first. In total, the Navy's acquisition strategy calls for three increments: mid-, low-, and high-band. The specific frequency ranges covered by these bands is classified.

Both federal statute and DOD policies include provisions designed to help prevent unnecessary duplication of investments. Section 2366a of title 10 of the U.S. Code provides that a major defense acquisition program may not receive milestone A approval until the Milestone Decision Authority certifies, after consultation with the Joint Requirements Oversight Council,

---

[8]Major defense acquisition programs are those identified by DOD that require eventual total research, development, test, and evaluation (RDT&E) expenditures, including all planned increments, of more than $365 million, or procurement expenditures, including all planned increments, of more than $2.19 billion, in fiscal year 2000 constant dollars.

[9]BAE Systems Information and Electronic Systems Integration Inc. filed a bid protest of the NGJ technology development contract award on July 18, 2013.

that if the program duplicates a capability already provided by an existing system, the duplication provided by such program is necessary and appropriate.[10] In addition, DOD's JCIDS Manual directs that initial capabilities documents, which describe capability gaps that require a materiel solution, identify proposed capability requirements for which there exists overlaps or redundancies.[11] Initial capabilities documents should also assess whether the overlap is advisable for operational redundancy or whether it should be evaluated as a potential trade-off or alternative to satisfy identified capability gaps. The manual also states that, when validating key requirements documents, the chair of the group responsible for that capability area is also certifying that the proposed requirements and capabilities are not unnecessarily redundant to existing capabilities in the joint force. This applies to initial capabilities documents, capability development documents, and capability production documents, which helps ensure that potential redundancies are discussed at multiple points in the acquisition process.

However, assessing duplication among airborne electronic attack investments is challenging for a variety of reasons. There is a lack of documentation comparing all current existing and planned airborne electronic attack capabilities; electronic warfare investments are distributed among the services; systems in the electronic warfare portfolio are classified at multiple levels; future needs and threats and plans to address them change quickly; planned programs of record or upgrades are not always known until funding is requested; and some overlap among systems is intentional.

---

[10]The Joint Requirements Oversight Council, which is chaired by the Vice Chairman of the Joint Chiefs of Staff, and includes one senior leader from each of the military services, among others, validates capability gaps and the requirements for the systems that are planned to address them.

[11]Department of Defense, *Manual for the Operation of the Joint Capabilities Integration and Development System* (Jan. 19, 2012). JCIDS validates gaps in joint warfighting capabilities and requirements that resolve those gaps.

DOD Analysis of Potential Duplication Does Not Address All NGJ Roles and Planned Acquisition Programs

DOD has assessed whether the planned NGJ program is duplicative using a variety of means, but none of them address all of the system's planned roles or take into account the military services' evolving airborne electronic attack investment plans. DOD's analyses of its airborne electronic attack capability gaps over the last decade, as well as the NGJ analysis of alternatives, support its conclusion that the NGJ is not duplicative of existing capabilities in its primary role – the joint suppression of enemy air defenses. However, these analyses do not address potential duplication or overlap between the NGJ and other systems being developed for other roles, such as communications jamming in irregular warfare environments. The military services also plan to invest in additional airborne electronic attack systems, so new duplication issues could emerge. Several ongoing DOD efforts could provide a mechanism for updating its analysis of potential overlap and duplication related to the NGJ. However, we found weaknesses in the execution of some of these efforts.

DOD Has Cited Its Assessments of Capability Gaps As Evidence That NGJ Is Not Duplicative

According to DOD and Joint Staff officials, the NGJ addresses a clear capability gap and is not duplicative of other airborne electronic attack systems. It is a direct replacement for the Navy's ALQ-99 tactical jamming system and addresses validated capability gaps. DOD analyses dating back a decade have identified capability gaps and provided a basis for service investments in airborne electronic attack capabilities, such as the NGJ. DOD outlined its findings in reports that included analyses of alternatives and initial capabilities documents.

None of these documents are specifically assessments of duplication; they serve other purposes. For example, the two initial capabilities documents – the 2004 Airborne Electronic Attack and 2009 Electronic Warfare Initial Capabilities Documents – identified the capability gaps that the NGJ is intended to address. Table 1 lists key documents and describes the extent to which they assessed duplication and overlap for NGJ.

Table 1: Key Documents and the Extent to Which They Considered Existing and Planned Capabilities and Assessed Duplication and Overlap for NGJ

Document	Consideration of duplication and overlap
2004 Airborne Electronic Attack Initial Capabilities Document	Assessed capability gaps. Does not directly address potential duplication and overlap.
2009 Electronic Warfare Initial Capabilities Document	Assessed capability gaps. Does not directly address potential duplication and overlap.
2011 NGJ Analysis of Alternatives	Considered existing and planned airborne electronic capabilities when determining the relative importance of targets that NGJ should address. Identified potential overlap and duplication among the targets that airborne electronic attack systems can address.

Source: GAO analysis of DOD documents.

According to DOD and Joint Staff officials, the analyses contained in these documents provided support for the certification the department is required to make that the NGJ is not unnecessarily duplicative before receiving milestone A approval to begin technology development. In addition, Joint Staff officials stated that they reviewed the NGJ and its potential capabilities for duplication before endorsing the NGJ Analysis of Alternatives. We were not able to review the Joint Staff's analysis due to its classification level.

DOD NGJ Analyses Do Not Reflect All of Its Planned Roles or Service Acquisition Plans

DOD analyses of NGJ capabilities and potential duplication do not reflect all of its planned roles, particularly in irregular warfare environments, or evolving service acquisition plans. Section 2366a of title 10 of the U.S. Code provides that a major defense acquisition program may not receive milestone A approval until the Milestone Decision Authority certifies, after consultation with the Joint Requirements Oversight Council, that if the program duplicates a capability already provided by an existing system, the duplication provided by such program is necessary and appropriate. DOD's analyses support its conclusion that the NGJ is not duplicative of existing capabilities in its primary role—the joint suppression of enemy air defenses in a modified escort setting, which includes defended airspace outside the range of known surface-to-air missiles. In fact, the NGJ Analysis of Alternatives found that the planned system would complement other DOD investments in electronic warfare and stealth. However, these analyses do not address potential duplication or overlap between the NGJ and systems being developed for other roles, such as communications jamming in irregular warfare environments—an area where we have found potential duplication in our prior work.[12] Most of these systems have been developed or incorporated into military service investment plans since these analyses were conducted.

Since the preparation of key NGJ-related documents, DOD has focused on increasing its airborne electronic attack capabilities and capacity, resulting in several systems that were not considered in those analyses. When these analyses were being completed, DOD had few airborne electronic attack systems and programs of record, none of which were specifically designed for the irregular warfare environment.[13] Table 2 shows existing and planned airborne electronic attack systems and whether they were discussed in key NGJ-related documents.

---

[12]GAO, *2012 Annual Report: Opportunities to Reduce Duplication, Overlap and Fragmentation, Achieve Savings, and Enhance Revenue*, GAO-12-342SP (Washington, D.C.: Feb. 28, 2012); and GAO-12-175.

[13]A program of record is a program that is included in the Future Years Defense Program—DOD's 5-year investment plan.

Table 2: Existing and Planned Airborne Electronic Attack Systems

Systems primarily for major combat operations	Primary role	Acquiring service	Status[a]	Existed or planned at the time of DOD's analyses
EC-130H	Stand-off, and communications jamming	Air Force	Existing	Yes
Miniature Air Launched Decoy-Jammer	Stand-in jamming	Air Force	Existing	Yes
Electronic Attack Enabled Active Electronically Scanned Array (AESA) Radar	Self protection; penetrating escort	Multiple	Planned	Yes
Next Generation Jammer	Stand-off, modified escort, and communications jamming	Navy	Planned	Yes
Multi-Platform Electronic Attack Pod Upgrade	Self protection/penetrating escort	Air Force	Planned	No
Systems primarily for irregular warfare				
Communications Electronic Attack with Surveillance and Reconnaissance (CEASAR)	Communications jamming	Army	Existing	No
Intrepid Tiger II Block 1	Communications jamming	Marine Corps	Existing	No
Multi-Function Electronic Warfare	Communications jamming	Army	Planned	No
Intrepid Tiger II Block X	Communications and radar jamming	Marine Corps	Planned	No

Source: GAO analysis of DOD documents and interviews with DOD officials.

Notes: Stand-off jamming occurs outside defended airspace.
Modified escort jamming occurs outside the known surface-to-air missile range.
Penetrating escort jamming occurs within known surface-to-air missile range.
Stand-in jamming occurs within the surface-to-air missile "no escape" zone.

[a]Planned systems only include those that are in the budget.

Based on our analysis of DOD airborne electronic attack systems and missions, none of the systems we reviewed that have emerged since DOD's NGJ analysis was completed duplicate planned capabilities; however, there is some overlap in the roles that the systems are intended to perform. For example, according to the F-35 program office, some aircraft with electronic attack enabled AESA radar may be able to perform some jamming functions in a modified escort role. However, unlike the NGJ, they are not designed to be dedicated jamming systems. In addition, NGJ is to be capable of communications jamming in an irregular warfare type environment, like systems such as CEASAR and Intrepid Tiger II, which were fielded under rapid acquisition authorities and in very limited quantities. Army and Marine Corps officials explained that their systems are a more suitable and economic alternative to the NGJ for these missions. For example, Army officials stated that the systems the

Army is investing in, such as CEASAR and Multi-Function Electronic Warfare, would provide the right amount of power for their needs, be more readily available to units, and cost less. According to DOD, these systems also provide additional capacity in an area where there has been significant demand. However, as DOD and the military services continue to invest in new additional airborne electronic attack capabilities, the potential for duplication and overlap to occur increases.

Ongoing DOD Efforts Provide Another Mechanism to Address Potential Overlap and Duplication

DOD has several ongoing efforts that could provide a mechanism for updating its analysis of potential overlap and duplication related to the NGJ and other airborne electronic attack investments, including its annual Electronic Warfare Strategy Report to Congress, a U.S. Strategic Command review of DOD's portfolio of electronic warfare systems, and the NGJ capability development document. However, we found weaknesses in two of the three efforts.

Electronic Warfare Strategy Report to Congress

DOD could address new duplication issues as they emerge and, if necessary, explain the need for overlapping capabilities in its electronic warfare strategy report to Congress. Section 1053 of the National Defense Authorization Act for Fiscal Year 2010 requires that for each of fiscal years 2011 through 2015, the Secretary of Defense, in coordination with the Joint Chiefs of Staff and secretaries of the military departments, submit to the congressional defense committees an annual report on DOD's electronic warfare strategy.[14] Each report must provide information on both unclassified and classified programs and projects, including whether or not the program or project is redundant or overlaps with the efforts of another military department.[15] DOD has produced two reports in response to this requirement. In these reports, DOD assessed duplication of airborne electronic attack systems, including NGJ. However, the analysis was limited and did not examine potential overlap between capabilities or explain why that overlap was warranted. DOD officials explained that the report relied primarily on the military services to self-identify overlap and duplication. Redundancy in some of these areas may, in fact, be desirable, but pursuing multiple acquisition efforts to develop similar capabilities can also result in the same capability gap being filled twice or more, which may contribute to other warfighting

---

[14]Pub. L. No. 111-84, §1053(a) (2009).

[15]Pub. L. No. 111-84, §1053(b) (2009).

needs going unfilled. This report is supposed to be submitted at the same time the President submits the budget to Congress, but DOD has not yet issued its report for fiscal year 2013 and could not provide a definitive date for when it plans to do so.

U.S. Strategic Command Annual Electronic Warfare Assessment

The U.S. Strategic Command also has an ongoing review that could help assess duplication and overlap issues related to the NGJ and other systems. Joint Staff officials stated that, during the course of our review, they began in collaboration with U.S. Strategic Command to review DOD's portfolio of electronic warfare systems at all levels of classification. They explained that the review will examine capability requirements in select approved warfighting scenarios as well as potential redundancy within the portfolio. According to the Joint Staff, the review should be completed sometime in fiscal year 2013.

NGJ Capability Development Document

Capability development documents, which define the performance requirements of acquisition programs, are another vehicle to discuss potential redundancies across proposed and existing programs. The Navy must produce and the Joint Requirements Oversight Council must validate a capability development document for the NGJ program before it can receive approval to enter system development—currently planned for fiscal year 2015. The JCIDS manual provides that, when validating capability development documents, the chair of the group responsible for that capability area is also certifying that the proposed requirements and capabilities are not unnecessarily redundant to existing capabilities in the joint force. The draft NGJ capability development document addresses potential redundancies by stating that the NGJ is fully synchronized with existing systems and will be synchronized with future systems, and that individual airborne electronic attack systems all concentrate on unique portions of the electromagnetic spectrum—frequency ranges—for different mission sets. However, the Navy did not identify the systems that it considered in its analysis, so it will be difficult for others to validate this conclusion or whether it applies to all of the NGJ's planned roles.

NGJ Capabilities Are to Support the Joint Force, but the Military Services Are Also Developing Systems Tailored to Their Specific Needs

The NGJ is not a joint acquisition program, but it is planned to provide airborne electronic attack capabilities that will support all military services in both major combat operations and irregular warfare environments. The NGJ is not intended to meet all of the military services' airborne electronic attack needs, and the services are planning to make additional investments in systems that are tailored to meet their specific warfighting roles. The military services may be able to leverage the NGJ program in support of their own acquisition priorities and programs because its current acquisition strategy is based on a modular open systems approach, which allows system components to be added, removed, modified, replaced, or sustained by different military customers or manufacturers without significantly impacting the remainder of the system. This approach could make it easier to integrate the NGJ or its technologies into other systems in the future.

NGJ Is Not a Joint Acquisition Program, but Its Capabilities Are to Support the Joint Force

Despite its role in joint military operations, the NGJ program is led and funded by the Navy and is not a joint acquisition program. The definition of a joint acquisition program is related to whether it is funded by more than one DOD component, not whether other organizations have provided input on it. In the case of the NGJ, the Joint Requirements Oversight Council, which is chaired by the Vice Chairman of the Joint Chiefs of Staff, and includes one senior leader from each of the military services, such as the Vice Chief of Staff of the Army or the Vice Chief of Naval Operations, has validated that the need exists for the program. The Marine Corps, Army, Air Force, and Joint Staff have provided input into the program as part of DOD's requirements and acquisition processes. This included collaboration on requirements documents and the NGJ Analysis of Alternatives. The Air Force's 2004 Airborne Electronic Attack Initial Capabilities Document and Strategic Command's 2009 Electronic Warfare Initial Capabilities Document, which informed NGJ requirements, included input from senior-level oversight boards representing all the military services. In addition, advisors from various parts of the Office of the Under Secretary of Defense, the Joint Staff, and all services provided input into the NGJ Analysis of Alternatives through forums such as working groups, integrated product teams, and a high-level executive steering committee.

DOD plans to use Navy EA-18Gs with the NGJ to support multiple military services in joint operational environments. In the joint operational environment, each service relies on the capabilities of the others to maximize its own effectiveness while minimizing its vulnerabilities. For example, in conducting military operations, U.S. aircraft are often at risk from enemy air defenses, such as surface-to-air missiles. EA-18Gs can use the NGJ jamming capabilities in these settings to disrupt enemy radar and communications and suppress enemy air defenses. Because aircraft, such as the EA-18G, are to protect aircraft of all services in hostile airspace, the joint suppression mission necessarily crosses individual service lines. The system the NGJ is replacing–ALQ-99–has also been used extensively in irregular warfare environments, including in Iraq and Afghanistan in response to electronic attack requests from all the military services.

Military Services Are Planning to Develop Additional Systems That Are Tailored to Their Roles

DOD has placed an emphasis on increasing airborne electronic attack capacity and capabilities. While the Navy's NGJ is expected to provide airborne electronic attack capabilities to support all military services in both major combat operations and irregular warfare environments, the other services are also planning to make additional investments in airborne electronic attack systems that are tailored to their specific warfighting roles. The services' airborne electronic attack plans vary in part because of these roles. For example, DOD officials explained that the Navy is responsible for ensuring freedom of navigation in the world's oceans and has a key role in force projection; the Marine Corps is a rapid expeditionary force; the Air Force provides long range strike and close air support and is responsible for establishing air superiority; and the Army is the primary force for land operations in war and usually enters a battle area after the Air Force has established air superiority. Military service officials characterized their airborne electronic attack plans and the role of the NGJ in them as follows:

- Air Force: The Air Force is focused on developing long range strike capabilities, enabling the electronic attack capabilities of its F-22A and F-35 aircraft for penetrating escort roles, and investing in improvements to self protection systems for its fighter aircraft, including the F-15 and the F-16. Air Force requirements officials stated that the planned capabilities of NGJ will complement the other systems it is developing.

- Army: Officials from the Army's Electronic Warfare Division stated that although the NGJ-equipped EA-18Gs would have a role in helping to establish air superiority before the Army enters an area, the Army plans to rely on its own airborne electronic attack systems to perform the necessary jamming in support of its ground forces. According to Army officials, the service plans to invest in less expensive, less powerful systems that will be readily available at the brigade combat team level. The Army developed CEASAR, a jamming pod on C-12 aircraft, and is now developing a more capable successor to CEASAR under the Multi-Function Electronic Warfare program, which is early in the acquisition process.

- Marine Corps: Officials from the Marine Corps' Electronic Warfare Branch stated that each Marine Air Ground Task Force commander must possess its own airborne electronic attack capabilities and the Marine Corps does not plan to rely solely on Navy EA-18G's with NGJ to support its air and ground forces. Historically, the Marines have relied on their own expeditionary EA-6B squadrons to meet joint electronic warfare requirements, but the EA-6Bs will be phased out by 2019 and the Marine Corps does not plan to acquire the EA-18G, which will be equipped with the NGJ. According to the Marine Corps, it will coordinate the use of NGJ support from the Navy when appropriate but it expects to rely on its own systems for its core missions. The Marine Corps plans to upgrade its Intrepid Tiger II jamming pods to support both communications and radar jamming, and develop a system to integrate air and ground electronic warfare units with other payloads designed to be used on any platform.

Open Systems Approach Could Facilitate Use of NGJ Technologies on Other Systems

The current acquisition strategy for the NGJ program calls for it to be integrated on one aircraft—the EA-18G—however, the program is planning on pursuing a modular open systems approach to development that could make it easier to integrate the NGJ or its technologies into other systems in the future. An open systems approach allows system components to be added, removed, modified, replaced, or sustained by the military customer or different manufacturers, in addition to the prime manufacturer that developed the system. It also allows independent suppliers to build components that can plug-in to the existing system through the open connections. Fundamental elements of an open systems approach include the following:

- Designing a system with modular components that isolate functionality. This makes the system easier to develop, maintain, and modify because components can be changed without significantly impacting the remainder of the system.

- Developing and using open, publicly available standards for the key interfaces, or connections, between the components.

According to NGJ program officials, a modular open systems approach would allow the NGJ to be designed so that it could adapt to threat and technology changes. It also enables future growth of the system. Furthermore, Navy officials stated that the approach could make it possible for NGJ components to be used and modified for application on significantly different platforms, including unmanned aerial vehicles. This approach is encouraged by DOD guidance, including its Better Buying Power initiative, as well as Navy guidance.

The NGJ Analysis of Alternatives also examined integrating the NGJ onto the F-35, which is being acquired by the Air Force, Marine Corp, and Navy, but the option was found to be too risky and costly for a near-term solution. Navy officials explained that, even with an open systems approach, integrating the NGJ with any platform is difficult. Even the integration associated with moving the ALQ-99 to the EA-18G was challenging. The cost of the effort was about $2 billion and took 5 years. Part of the integration challenge was adapting the operator workload system because the EA-6B is a four-operator aircraft while the EA-18G is a two-operator aircraft. The F-35 is a single-operator aircraft, which officials explained would cause significant integration challenges for the NGJ.

Conclusions

Airborne electronic attack is an important enabling capability for U.S. military forces in both major combat operations and irregular warfare environments. In response to rapidly evolving threats and mission needs, DOD is making investments to increase both its airborne electronic attack capacity and capabilities. At an estimated cost of over $7 billion, the NGJ represents a significant investment in airborne electronic attack capabilities. Investments of this size must be well-justified and are required by statute and DOD policy to be examined for unnecessary redundancy. DOD's analysis of its airborne electronic attack capability gaps over the last decade, as well as the NGJ analysis of alternatives, supports its conclusion that the NGJ meets a valid need and is not duplicative of existing capabilities in its primary role. However, in the time since DOD completed some of these analyses, the investment plans of the military services have changed, particularly in the irregular warfare area. The military services are quick to differentiate their airborne electronic attack needs and justify individual service, rather than joint or common, solutions to meet them. While none of the new programs planned duplicate NGJ capabilities, new areas of overlap and potential duplication could emerge as these plans continue to evolve. Redundancy in some of these areas may, in fact, be desirable, but pursuing multiple acquisition efforts to develop similar capabilities can also result in the same capability gap being filled twice or more, lead to inefficient use of resources, and contribute to other warfighting needs going unfilled.

DOD has mechanisms, such as the Electronic Warfare Strategy Report to Congress, U.S. Strategic Command Annual Electronic Warfare Assessment, and NGJ capability development document, that it can use to continue to assess overlap and duplication between the NGJ and other airborne electronic capabilities at key points in the acquisition process and communicate its evolving airborne electronic attack investment plans to Congress. Identifying existing and planned systems across all of the NGJ's planned roles in its capability development document could help ensure that DOD's analysis of potential overlap and duplication is complete. Moreover, providing Electronic Warfare Strategy Reports to Congress as required and incorporating information on potentially overlapping systems and why such overlap is warranted would provide Congress with more complete information about the relationship between electronic warfare programs.

Recommendations for Executive Action

We recommend that the Secretary of Defense take the following two actions:

- To help ensure that the NGJ does not unnecessarily duplicate existing or planned capabilities, require the Navy, in coordination with the Joint Staff, to address overlap and duplication between the NGJ and other systems in all of its planned roles in the NGJ capability development document. The NGJ capability development document should identify the existing and planned systems that the Navy assessed for potential redundancies to help determine if its analysis was comprehensive.

- To provide Congress complete information about the relationship between electronic warfare programs, ensure that the Electronic Warfare Strategy Reports to Congress include information on potentially overlapping capabilities among systems, such as the NGJ and Electronically Attack Enabled AESA Radar, CEASAR, Intrepid Tiger II, and Multi-Function Electronic Warfare, and why that overlap is warranted.

Agency Comments and Our Evaluation

We provided a draft of this report to DOD for review and comment. In its written comments, which are reprinted in full in appendix II, DOD partially concurred with our first recommendation and concurred with our second recommendation. DOD also provided technical comments that were incorporated as appropriate.

DOD partially concurred with our recommendation to address overlap and duplication between the NGJ and other systems in all of its planned roles in the NGJ capability development document. DOD responded that it concurs with the need to continue to assess unnecessary duplication and redundancy, but it does not concur with including the assessment in the capability development document. Rather DOD stated that it will address unnecessary duplication and redundancy in accordance with its existing processes, such as the Joint Capabilities Integration Development System (JCIDS), and statutory requirements. DOD explained that changes it made to the JCIDS process in January 2012 address the concerns about potential capability overlaps and redundancies raised in this and other GAO reports. For example, the revised JCIDS manual emphasized the role of functional capabilities board in assessing potential unnecessary capability redundancy prior to forwarding a program's requirements documents for approval. In addition, DOD stated that the Joint Staff is further improving these processes through a pending update to JCIDS that will include increased emphasis on functional area portfolio management. DOD also reiterated in its comments and in a classified enclosure that NGJ's capabilities are not unnecessarily duplicative.

We acknowledged the existing JCIDS mechanisms that address potential overlap and duplication in this report and have discussed the value of effective portfolio management in prior reports. However, as we point out in our recommendation, documenting the assessments that support these processes is important because it allows others to determine if DOD's analysis was comprehensive. We identified the NGJ capability development document as the appropriate vehicle to document DOD's assessment of potential duplication because DOD already requires that potential overlap and duplication be considered before the document can be validated and the program can move forward in the acquisition process. Finally, while DOD's current analysis indicates that none of its current or planned programs duplicate NGJ capabilities, new areas of overlap and potential duplication could emerge as military service investment plans continue to evolve.

DOD concurred with our second recommendation regarding providing complete information about the relationship between electronic warfare programs in its Electronic Warfare Strategy Reports to Congress. DOD did not provide details regarding how it plans to implement this recommendation.

We are sending copies of this report to interested congressional committees, the Secretary of Defense, the Secretary of the Army, the Secretary of the Navy, the Secretary of the Air Force, and the Commandant of the Marine Corps. In addition, the report is available at no charge on the GAO website at http://www.gao.gov.

If you or your staff have any questions about this report, please contact me at (202) 512-4841 or sullivanm@gao.gov. Contact points for our Offices of Congressional Relations and Public Affairs may be found on the last page of this report. GAO staff who made key contributions to this report are listed in appendix III.

Michael J. Sullivan
Director
Acquisition and Sourcing Management

Appendix I: Scope and Methodology

To determine the extent to which the Department of Defense (DOD) assessed duplication among the Next Generation Jammer (NGJ), existing capabilities, and other acquisition programs, we reviewed key NGJ and DOD electronic warfare documents, including the 2004 Airborne Electronic Attack Initial Capabilities Document, the 2009 Electronic Warfare Initial Capabilities Document, the NGJ Analysis of Alternatives (AOA), and the DOD Annual Electronic Warfare Strategy Report to Congress, to determine whether potential duplication was considered as DOD developed NGJ requirements and prepared for initiation of the NGJ acquisition program. We interviewed DOD, military service, and program officials and the Joint Staff about how these analyses were conducted. We assessed DOD's analysis of duplication against DOD's Joint Capabilities Integration and Development System (JCIDS) Manual.[1] In addition, we reviewed information up to the SECRET level provided by the military services regarding the capabilities and missions of existing and planned airborne electronic attack systems. Our analysis was limited to non-kinetic airborne electronic attack systems as opposed to kinetic capabilities which focus on destroying forces through the application of physical effects.

To determine the extent to which the NGJ is being managed as a joint solution, we reviewed key requirements and acquisition documents reflecting military service and Joint Staff input into NGJ requirements and the acquisition program. We also interviewed DOD, military service, and program officials to determine the extent to which the military services provided input into NGJ requirements and the acquisition program. In addition, we analyzed documents, such as memorandums of agreement among the military services, and interviewed military service and Joint Staff officials to obtain an understanding of how NGJ is expected to operate in the joint force. We also reviewed the NGJ AOA and interviewed program officials to determine if the system is intended to be used on multiple platforms.

We conducted this performance audit from November 2012 to August 2013 in accordance with generally accepted government auditing standards. Those standards require that we plan and perform the audit to obtain sufficient, appropriate evidence to provide a reasonable basis for

---

[1]Department of Defense. *Manual for the Operation of the Joint Capabilities Integration and Development System* (Jan. 19, 2012).

our findings and conclusions based on our audit objectives. Our analysis was also limited to information classified no higher than SECRET, but we believe that the evidence obtained provides a reasonable basis for our findings and conclusions based on our audit objectives.

Appendix II: Comments from the Department of Defense

ASSISTANT SECRETARY OF DEFENSE
3015 DEFENSE PENTAGON
WASHINGTON, DC 20301-3015

ACQUISITION

080613

Mr. Mike Sullivan
Director, Acquisition and Sourcing Management
U.S. Government Accountability Office
441 G Street, N.W.
Washington, DC 20548

Dear Mr. Sullivan:

This is the Department of Defense response to the GAO Draft Report, GAO-13-642, "NEXT GENERATION JAMMER: DoD Should Continue to Assess Potential Duplication and Overlap as Program Moves Forward," dated July 3, 2013 (GAO Code 121103). The Department acknowledges receipt of the draft report.

As more fully explained in the UNCLASSIFIED Enclosure 1 and SECRET Enclosure 2, the Department partially concurs with recommendation one and concurs with recommendation two.

The Department appreciates the opportunity to comment on the draft report. For further questions concerning this report, please contact Mr. Ronald Woods, OUSD(AT&L)/Acting Director for Air Warfare, Ronald.Woods@osd.mil or 703-697-8183.

Sincerely,

Katrina McFarland

Enclosures:
As stated

Regrade UNCLASSIFIED when separated from enclosure

Enclosure 1

GAO DRAFT REPORT DATED JULY 3, 2013
GAO-13-642 (GAO CODE 121103)

"NEXT GENERATION JAMMER: DOD SHOULD CONTINUE TO ASSESS
POTENTIAL DUPLICATION AND OVERLAP AS PROGRAM MOVES FORWARD,"

DEPARTMENT OF DEFENSE COMMENTS
TO THE GAO RECOMMENDATION

RECOMMENDATION 1: To help ensure that NGJ does not unnecessarily duplicate existing or planned capabilities, require the Navy, in coordination with the Joint Staff, to address overlap and duplication between the NGJ and other systems in all of its planned roles in the NGJ capability development document. The NGJ capability development document should identify the existing and planned systems that the Navy assessed for potential redundancies to help determine if its analysis was comprehensive.

DoD RESPONSE: Partially concur. The Department agrees that we should continue to assess unnecessarily duplication and redundancy and will in accordance with our documented processes and statutory requirements. As the GAO highlights, DoD analyses support our conclusion that NGJ is not duplicative in its primary role – suppression of enemy air defenses. The Department concurs and clarifies that NGJ's primary role is the _Joint_ Suppression of Enemy Air Defenses (JSEAD). DoD has no other platforms/systems that provide airborne electronic attack capabilities in this frequency range with the high power levels and high duty cycles of the NGJ.

High power levels and high duty cycles are required to be effective in the JSEAD mission, NGJ's most stressing role, and JSEAD is the primary driver of the system's design. NGJ's additional roles – such as counter-communications, counter-radio-controlled improvised explosive device, counter-position, navigation and timing, and counter-targeting – come at negligible cost because they do not drive the system's design, and these roles meet validated Navy specific and Joint mission requirements. Removing these additional roles from the NGJ program would not reduce program costs, but would force the Navy to procure another pod for the communications jamming mission. Thus what GAO identifies as potential duplication, the Department believes is an efficient use of resources to increase communications jamming capacity to meet validated warfighting requirements. The Department believes its previous works substantiate its current plans as outlined above and further detailed in the classified Enclosure 2.

The GAO also suggests the Navy and Joint Staff should identify and address all other systems that appear to overlap or duplicate any one of the many capabilities NGJ brings to the fight in all of NGJ's planned roles in the NGJ capabilities development document (CDD). The Department concurs with the need to assess unnecessary duplication and redundancy, but does not concur that including this assessment in the CDD is appropriate. The update of the Joint Capability Integration and Development System (JCIDS) in January of 2012 addressed many of the GAO's concerns listed in this and previous GAO reports (GAO 11-502 and 12-175) which also recommended improving JCIDS to better account for potential capability overlaps and redundancies. Some of these changes include the mandate for Services to document their rapidly developed capabilities in the knowledge management/decision support tool, the central data

UNCLASSIFIED

repository used by the JCIDS systems, and emphasizing the Functional Capabilities Board role in assessing potential unnecessary capability redundancy prior to forwarding documents for Joint Requirements Oversight Council validation. The Joint Staff is further improving these processes through a pending update to the JCIDS process to include increased emphasis on functional area portfolio management.

RECOMMENDATION 2: To provide Congress complete information about the relationship between electronic warfare programs, ensure that the Electronic Warfare Strategy Reports to Congress includes information on potentially overlapping capabilities among systems, such as the NGJ and Electronically Attack Enabled AESA Radar, CEASAR, Intrepid Tiger II, and Multi-Function Electronic Warfare, and why that overlap is warranted.

DoD RESPONSE: Concur.

2

UNCLASSIFIED

Appendix III: GAO Contact and Staff Acknowledgments

GAO Contact	Michael J. Sullivan, (202) 512-4841 or sullivanm@gao.gov
Acknowledgments	In addition to the contact named above, the following individuals made key contributions to this report: Ronald E. Schwenn, Assistant Director; Teakoe Coleman; Laura Greifner; John Krump; Laura Holliday; Brian Lepore; Anh Nguyen; Madhav Panwar; Mark Pross; and Roxanna Sun.

(121103)